The Great Wall, a remarkable symbol of the Chinese nation and its civilization, embodies the unremitting pursuit of self-improvement and the patriotic sentiments of unity and perseverance among the Chinese people.

长城是中华民族的代表性符号和中华文明的重要象征，凝聚着中华民族自强不息的奋斗精神和众志成城、坚韧不屈的爱国情怀。

北京司马台长城 1998 Simatai Great Wall, Beijing, 1998

Prologue: The Poems of Civilization, The Mirror of the World

The encounter of civilizations is never merely a historical accident; it represents humanity's eternal pursuit of mutual understanding and symbiosis. By capturing the rustic bricks and stones of the Great Wall through his lens, Michael Yamashita not only reproduces history through light and shadow but also engages in a dialogue between civilizations that transcends time and space. Through his travels spanning over forty years and covering hundreds of thousands of kilometers, this photographer from the West has established a channel for communication between the East and the West. By traversing vast landscapes and tracing a long history, he has documented the Great Wall through a Western perspective, transforming its grandeur, vastness, resilience, and tenderness into a universal language that the world can comprehend.

The Great Wall serves as a spiritual totem for the Chinese people and embodies the civilizational genes etched into the Chinese landscape. It reflects the broader tapestry of world civilization. The rammed earth walls on the Loess Plateau illustrate the wisdom of agrarian societies. The beacon fires and the sound of camel bells along the Hexi Corridor resonate with the vibrant trade of the Silk Road. The steepness of the Wall at Jiankou stands as a testament to the enduring struggle between humanity and nature.

As an Eastern spiritual totem meeting Western photographic language, the Great Wall transcends its status as merely a "historical relic"; it becomes a "prism" through which global audiences can understand China. By examining photographs composed according to the golden ratio, Western viewers are awed by the magnificence of this human-made structure and draw inspiration from its embodiment of courage and perseverance. Meanwhile, Eastern scholars uncover signs of ecological change within these photographic archives, gaining insights into self-awareness that are both familiar and novel. Yamashita's images reconstruct the spiritual atlas of the "Great Wall stories" at present, which undoubtedly belong to both China and the world. Such a Chinese narrative is no longer a one-way exportation; it evolves into a medium for dialogue, inviting global audiences to participate and reflect. This "two-way decoding" narrative encapsulates the essence of "East Meets West": it is not aimed at cultural conquest but focuses on the mission of value symbiosis.

For over a decade, the Reignwood Culture Foundation has been moving forward with the notion of "East Meets West." We fully recognize that this does not simply mean a one-way exportation but serves as a signpost for dialogue among civilizations. Through systematic efforts in image preservation, we transform scattered photo negatives into the collective memory of the Chinese people, fulfilling our mission of fostering cultural dialogue. As the Foundation's founder, Mr. Yan Bin, always advocates: "the encounter of civilizations is about allowing the world to see China and enabling China to see itself through the eyes of the world."

This photo book, *Encountering the Great Wall*, centers on the Wall and serves as both an echo of history and a prologue to the future. It invites Eastern and Western cultures to merge through their interactions and to experience a rebirth through dialogue. We aim to take the publication of this book as a starting point, employing images as our vessel to convey the civilizational codes of the Tea-Horse Road, the Grand Canal, and the Silk Road to the world. As readers worldwide peruse these pages, they will not just witness the majestic landscapes of China but hear the harmonious resonance of diverse civilizations. While bricks and stones may remain silent, light and shadow tell their stories. The mountains and rivers know no boundaries, and the paths of civilizations will inevitably cross again.

The beacon fires of the Great Wall have long vanished, but the spark of civilization will forever endure.

Reignwood Culture Foundation
March 2025

序：文明的诗篇 世界的镜像

文明的相遇，从来不是历史的偶然，而是人类对理解与共生的永恒追寻。当麦克·山下（Michael Yamashita）的镜头穿越长城砖石的褶皱，这不仅是光影对历史的复刻，更是一场跨越时空的文明对话。这位来自西方的摄影师，以其跨越四十余载的行走、数十万公里的凝视，架设起了一条东西方对话的桥梁。在西方镜头语言的记录下，他穿越山河、叩击岁月，将长城的雄浑与苍茫、坚韧与温情，转化为世界可感可知的共通语言。

长城，是中华民族的精神图腾，是镌刻在华夏大地上的文明基因，亦是世界文明的镜像：黄土高原的夯土墙垣诉说着农耕文明的智慧，河西走廊的烽燧驼铃回荡着丝路贸易的繁华，箭扣长城的险峻奇崛则见证着人类与自然的永恒博弈。

当西方摄影语言与东方精神图腾相遇，长城跳脱出“历史遗迹”的单一符号，转而成为全球观众理解中国的“多棱镜”：西方观众从黄金分割构图中感叹这项人类工程的壮美，从中品悟勇气与坚守；东方学者在影像档案里发现生态变迁的密码，洞察熟悉而新鲜的自我认知。麦克·山下的影像在当下重构了“长城故事”的精神图谱——它属于中国，亦属于世界。中国故事不再是单向的输出，而成为全球观众可参与、可反思的对话载体。这种“双向解码”的叙事，正是“当东方遇见西方”的核心：不以文化征服为目标，而以价值共生为使命。

华彬文化基金会十余年来以“当东方遇见西方”为理念前行，我们深知这不是单向输出的标识，而是文明对话的路标。通过体系化的影像保护工程，令散落的底片终成中国人的集体记忆，正是对这份文化对话使命的躬身践行。恰如基金会发起人严彬先生所倡导的：“文明的相遇，是让世界看见中国，也让中国看见世界眼中的自己。”

《遇见长城》以长城为轴，是历史的回响，亦是未来的序章；让东西方文化在碰撞中交融，在对话中新生。我们愿以此为起点，以影像为舟，载着茶马古道、大运河、丝绸之路的文明密码驶向世界。当世界各地的指尖拂过这些书页，人们不仅能看见中国的山河，更能听见文明的和鸣——因为砖石沉默，但光影会说话；山河无界，而文明终将相遇。

长城的烽火早已熄灭，但文明的火种，永远炽热。

华彬文化基金会
2025年3月

Preface

China has been my subject for the last 40 years, and the reason is that during that time, the most interesting things in the world seemed to be happening here. China has been for me the most exciting place in the world. As China's greatest icon, the Great Wall has been at the top of every visitor's bucket list. This was certainly the case for me on my first trip to China in 1982.

Of course, the Chinese people are my primary audience, but the rest of the world deserves to see the history of China that I have been recording during its biggest growth years.

Among the most fortuitous experiences I've had while covering China was meeting Mr. Yan Bin and the Reignwood Culture Foundation in 2015. Our collaboration is a perfect marriage because of our mutual mission of "East Meets West". And thanks to the Chairman and Reignwood, these pictures now have a life and can be seen by thousands of people.

I would like to extend my heartfelt thanks to Mr. Yan Bin for his vision and his efforts to bring the world closer together through this book and Reignwood's many "East Meets West" events.

Michael Yamashita
October,2024

前言

我摄影职业生涯四十余年的拍摄主题都与中国有关，那是因为世界上最有趣的事情都发生在这里，中国是世界上最令人兴奋的地方。长城作为中华民族的精神图腾，始终镌刻在每位旅人的夙愿清单之巅。1982 年我初到中国时，亦是如此——那时的我把登上长城视为最重要的人生体验。

我的镜头定格了中国腾飞年代的光影瞬间，华夏儿女自是最珍视的知音，寰宇众生亦当共鉴这份历史长卷。

所幸因缘际会，2015 年得遇严彬先生与华彬文化基金会。“当东方遇见西方”之理念，恰是我们共同的追求。这些尘封的影像终获新生。

请允许我向严彬先生致以诚挚的敬意——感谢他的远见卓识和大力支持，通过“当东方遇见西方”的开创性项目，架起了连接世界的文化桥梁。

麦克·山下
2024 年 10 月

TEN THOUSAND MILES OF LANDSCAPES

山河万里

长城，作为中华大地的脉络和象征，横亘在广袤的山河之间，见证了千年的风云变幻。本篇章以壮丽的景观摄影为主，展现长城沿线的各式风貌。从北国的严寒荒原到南方的青山绿水，长城的形态与自然环境融为一体，承载着深厚的历史记忆。每一段墙体，都仿佛在诉说着一个古老的故事；每一处曲折的城墙，都是历史的烙印。本篇章意在通过影像传递长城与山河的密切关系，探索长城作为自然与文化相交汇的巨大象征，在中国版图中的独特地位与文化意义。

As a vein and a symbol of China, the Great Wall stretches across vast mountains and rivers, witnessing the country's changes over thousands of years. This chapter primarily features stunning landscape photography, presenting the diverse scenes along the Great Wall. From the frigid wilderness in the north to the lush mountains and clear waters in the south, the structure of the Great Wall blends into the natural surroundings, carrying indelible memories of the past. Each segment of the winding wall seems to be telling an ancient story and bears the marks of history. This chapter aims to illuminate the close relationship between the Great Wall and the landscapes through images and to explore its unique status and cultural significance within Chinese territory, as it stands at the intersection of nature and culture.

河北山海关老龙头，2008 年 Laolongtou Great Wall, Shanhaiguan Pass Scenic Spot, Hebei, 2008

山海关，长城与渤海相接的地方，名副其实的『天下第一关』。20世纪80年代重建之后，它看上去就像人们所期望的长城的样子：高大、雄伟，对任何想要去到另一边的人来说都是一道不容小觑的屏障，除了渔民。长城入海处叫『老龙头』，我们坐在一旁的沙滩上，看着至少十几艘渔船在离岸四五十米的海域绕圈。大多数船上都载着渔民，他们拖着网从海底捕捞螃蟹。向导告诉我们，正是长城的水下遗存使得这一区域的海洋生物格外丰富。我很高兴亲眼目睹长城在今天得到有效利用。当天下午晚些时候，山海关又充当了我拍摄教师合唱队为业余歌唱比赛排练的背景。长城的声学作用无疑提升了歌唱效果，歌声在砖墙上回荡，为教师们演唱中国国歌增添了共鸣。缀有金黄色党徽图案的一面面红旗在风中飘扬，恰如其分地构成了象征中国的色彩强调。

——**摄影师手记**

河北潘家口西腾口段水下长城，2001年 Panjiakou Underwater Great Wall, Hebei, 2001

Shanhaiguan, where the Wall meets the waters of the Bohai Sea, literally means "First Pass Under Heaven." Rebuilt in the 1980s, it looks as one expects the Great Wall to look, massive and formidable, a truly imposing barrier to anyone wanting to get to the other side, except for the fishermen.We sat on the beach where the part of the Wall known as Laolongtou (Old Dragon's Head) meets the sea, watching at least a dozen fishing boats circling an area 50 yards off shore. Most of the boats carried fishermen, dragging nets along the bottom for crabs. Our guides told us that it is the remains of the Wall below the surface that make this area especially rich in sea life. I was glad to witness my first example of the Wall being put to good uses today. Later that afternoon, Shanhaiguan also served as a backdrop to some pictures I took of a teachers' choral group practicing for an amateur song contest. And the singing was certainly improved by the Wall's acoustics, as voices bounced off the brick, giving a resonating boost to the teachers' rendition of China's national anthem. Red and yellow hammer and sickle flags fluttered in the wind, a fitting splash of color emphasis for the symbol of China.

——Photographer's Notes

河北潘家口西腾口段水下长城，2001 年 Panjiakou Underwater Great Wall, Hebei, 2001

北京八达岭长城，1998 年　Badaling Great Wall, Beijing, 1998

摄影师很贪婪，他们永远不知道何时该停下来。如果你没有看到，你就无法拍摄。如果你看到了却没有拍摄，你就会失之交臂。只要有一线希望找到新的拍摄角度，我就会去探索。对我来说，司马台和金山岭之间的那段长城是最理想的，也是最出片的。这段十几公里的长城，有不下三十座烽火台、多处急转弯和陡峭的垂直爬升，你需要花一整天来充分欣赏（快步走的话需四五个钟头，还不包括停下来拍照的时间），才能感受光线在风景上呈现的完整变化。

——**摄影师手记**

北京司马台长城，2003 年 Simatai Great Wall, Beijing , 2003

Photographers are greedy; they never know when to stop. If you don't see it, you can't shoot it. If you don't shoot it when you see it, you've missed it. Wherever there was even a chance of a new angle, I set out to investigate. After seeking out all the Walls, for my money, the stretch between Simatai and Jinshanling is the best, the most photogenic. You need a full day to completely appreciate the eight or nine miles with over thirty watchtowers, switchbacks and steep vertical climbs (four to five hours at a brisk hiking pace, and that's without stopping for pictures) to see the effects of the total range of light over the landscape.

——**Photographer's Notes**

北京司马台长城，2003 年 Simatai Great Wall, Beijing , 2003

河北金山岭长城，2002 年 Jinshanling Great Wall, Hebei, 2002

河北金山岭长城，2007 年　Jinshanling Great Wall, Hebei, 2007

越过金山岭长城出口，再爬上几座烽火台，便可看到经典的长城画面：前景中的烽火台，从画面各个角落蜿蜒而出的S形城墙，以及远处山峰上如龙脊一般锯齿状的司马台长城。这一切，构成了日落时分、魔幻时刻的完美画面，也为我在长城上度过的令人惊叹的一天画上了完美句点。

——摄影师手记

河北金山岭长城，1998年 Jinshanling Great Wall, Hebei, 1998

Hiking a few more towers, above and beyond the Jinshanling Wall exit, there was the classic Wall shot: watchtower in foreground, serpentine s-curving walls extending from each corner of the frame, and the jagged dragon-backed peaks of Simatai in the far distance completing the picture at sunset's magic hour. It was a fitting end to an awe-inspiring day on the Wall.

——**Photographer's Notes**

河北金山岭长城，2005 年 Jinshanling Great Wall, Hebei, 2005

长城通常是游客在北京近郊游览的首选之地，也往往是每个人中国之旅中最精彩、最难忘的部分。对我来说当然也不例外。作为一名亚洲专家和为《国家地理》杂志工作了40年的摄影师，自1982年年第一次出差中国以来，我已多次参观长城。在随后的工作中，随着我对横亘北中国的各段长城进行拍摄，特别是沿着丝绸之路拍摄甘肃段长城，我对它如同游龙般蜿蜒于广袤大地产生了不可名状的欣赏。第一次中国行之后我便意识到，总有一天，我会向《国家地理》杂志的编辑们提交一篇关于长城的报道。在首次踏上这片土地20年后，我感觉时机已经成熟。

——**摄影师手记**

北京箭扣长城，2002年 Jiankou Great Wall, Beijing, 2002

The Great Wall is generally the first place outside Beijing that tourists visit, and it is usually the highlight and most memorable part of everyone's trip to China. It certainly was for me. As an Asia specialist and photographer working for the *National Geographic* for 40 years, I've visited the Great Wall many times since my first trip on assignment to China in 1982. On subsequent assignments, as I photographed other sections of the Wall across northern China, particularly along the Silk Road in Gansu, I developed a wondrous appreciation for the length and breadth of its geography as it snakes its way through the landscape. I knew after that first trip that it was only a matter of time before I would propose a story on the Wall to my editors at the *National Geographic*. Twenty years after my first visit, I decided the time was right.

——Photographer's Notes

北京居庸关长城，2007 年 Juyongguan Great Wall, Beijing, 2007

北京居庸关长城，1998 年
Juyongguan Great Wall, Beijing, 1998

北京司马台长城望京楼，1998 年
Wangjinglou Tower of Simatai Great Wall, Beijing, 1998

北京八达岭长城，1982 年 Badaling Great Wall, Beijing, 1982

北京八达岭长城，2008 年 Badaling Great Wall, Beijing, 2008

陕西榆林镇北台，2001 年 Zhenbeitai Tower, Yulin, Shaanxi, 2001

甘肃乌鞘岭，2001 年　Wushaoling, Gansu, 2001

甘肃乌鞘岭，2002 年　Wushaoling, Gansu, 2002

甘肃嘉峪关，2002 年　Jiayuguan, Gansu, 2002

我发现，关于长城的错误信息数不胜数。原来，这些错误信息大多出自《国家地理》此前唯一一篇关于长城的报道，文章发表于1923年2月，题为《沿着中国长城的千里之行》（*A Thousand Miles Along the Great Wall of China*）。这篇32页的报道开篇便提到了一则流传甚广的有关长城的说法——『从月球上唯一能用肉眼看到的人造之物就是中国的长城。』如今我们都知道，事实并非如此。

——**摄影师手记**

甘肃夏口，2002年 Xiakou, Gansu, 2002

I discovered there's virtually no limit to the misinformation out there about the Great Wall. As it turns out, much of that misinformation came from the only other story the *National Geographic* had published on the Wall, which appeared in the February, 1923 issue, entitled "*A Thousand Miles Along the Great Wall of China.*" That 32-page story leads with the most widely believed myth about the Wall… "*the only work of man's hands which would be visible to the human eye from the moon is the Great Wall of China.*" That, as we all now know, is certainly not the case.

—— **Photographer's Notes**

甘肃黄土高原上的墙与沙漠，2002 年 Wall and Desert, Loess Plateau, Gansu , 2002

甘肃嘉峪关，2001 年 Jiayuguan, Gansu, 2001

汉长城的城堡遗址，1998 年 The castle ruins of the Han Great Wall, 1998

甘肃河西走廊，2001 年　Great Wall, Hexi Corridor, Gansu, 2001

长城最伟大的地方在于它所穿越的辽阔地域，它曾是华夏帝国最北的边界，我觉得最吸引我拍摄的就是这个正在迅速发展的中国，这个我在1982年年首次到访时就爱上的中国。

——摄影师手记

宁夏三关口，2007年 San Guan Kou, Ningxia, 2007

The greatest thing about the Wall is the geography of the lands it travels through. It is this China that I find most compelling for pictures, the traditional China that is fast developing, the China I fell in love with when I first visited in 1982.

——**Photographer's Notes**

河西走廊祁连山脉，2007 年 Hexi Corridor and Qilian Mountains, 2007

甘肃嘉峪关，2001 年 Jiayuguan, Gansu, 2001

甘肃嘉峪关，2002 年 Jiayuguan, Gansu, 2002

不过，我的报道提案还是得以通过。任务很简单：沿着长城，从其位于中朝边界的起点一直走到位于塔克拉玛干沙漠的终点，并拜访那些修建和保卫过长城的人的后裔。于是在2001年年秋天，我开启了探寻真正的长城的个人旅程。

——**摄影师手记**

嘉峪关北大河，2000年 Beida River near Jiayuguan, 2000

My story proposal nevertheless passed muster. The assignment was simple: Follow the Great Wall from its beginning at the North Korean border to its end in the Taklilmakhan desert and meet the people whose ancestors built and defended the Wall. So I began my personal journey in the fall of 2001, in search of the real Great Wall.

——**Photographer's Notes**

甘肃玉门关，2001 年 Yumenguan, Gansu, 2001

HUSTLE AND BUSTLE OF THE LIVING WORLD

烟火人间

长城不仅是石砌的建筑，更是沿线人们生活的一部分，是历史与当下、人与自然交织的缩影。本篇章通过影像记录了长城脚下人们的生活点滴，从农田到集市，从家庭到村落，展现了长城与周边社区的日常共生。人们在这片历史遗迹中劳作、生活、传承，不仅是大自然与历史的守望者，也是文化与传统的传递者。每一张照片都承载着一段朴实的故事，展现了在这片古老土地上，人们如何在现代化浪潮中坚守着与长城共同的根脉和温情。

The Great Wall is not just a structure built with stones; it is also a part of people's lives, a microcosm interwoven with history and the present, as well as man and nature. The photos in this chapter capture the daily life of people at the foot of the Great Wall, from farmlands to markets and families to villages, showing the everyday symbiosis between the Great Wall and the surrounding communities. In the vicinity of the historical remains, people work, live, and pass their legacies down to every generation. They are the guardians of nature and history and, by all means, the conveyors of culture and tradition. Each photo tells an unadorned story, showing how the people of this ancient land adhere to the roots and warmth they share with the Great Wall in the tide of modernization.

辽宁丹东宽甸，2001 年 Kuandian County, Dandong, Liaoning, 2001

辽宁丹东宽甸，2001 年
Kuandian County, Dandong, Liaoning, 2001

辽宁丹东宽甸，2001 年
Kuandian County, Dandong, Liaoning, 2001

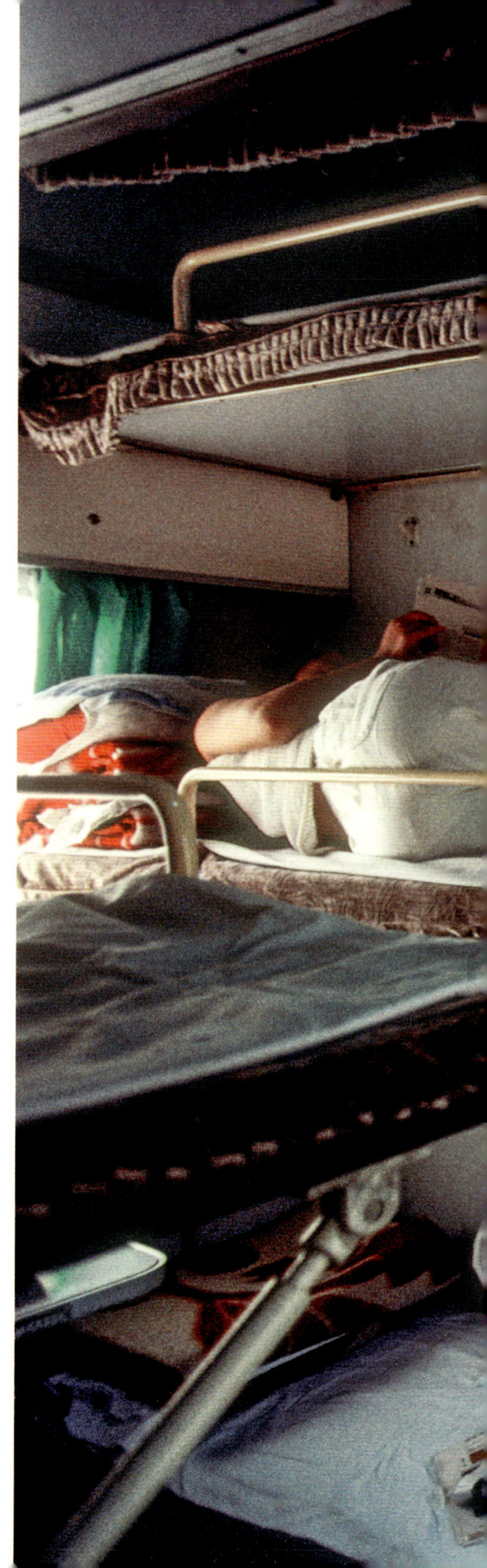

北京至丹东卧铺列车，2001 年　Sleeper train from Beijing to Dandong, 2001

离开山海关，我们循着落日，沿长城继续西行。长城在群山和山谷间蜿蜒起伏，穿过村庄和农田，直到再次消失在水中。这次是淡水，它没入潘家口水库，形成水下长城景观。

——**摄影师手记**

河北山海关，2001 年 Shanhaiguan, Hebei, 2001

Leaving Shanhaiguan, we followed the route of the Wall west, relying on the setting sun as our guide. The Wall undulates over mountains and valleys, between villages and farmland. We continued following the Wall until it once again disappeared into water this time fresh water, into the man-made reservoir of Panjiakou.

——Photographer's Notes

河北潘家口，2002 年 Panjiakou, Hebei, 2002

我站在水库中一座小岛露出的城墙顶上，拍摄了一位渔民划船越过水下长城段的情景。在他身后，长城再次浮出水面，跃上群山，主宰大地，随后蜿蜒而去。

看着他，我不禁想，这些世世代代生活在内陆省份、远离大海的农民，从来没有乘过船，也没有学过游泳，怎么能够一下子适应在大湖上的生活？但他们的确适应了，而且，对他们中的大多数人来说，捕鱼似乎比务农更有吸引力，也更有利可图。而这面湖、众多的渔家小馆以及长城本身，无不吸引着来自北京的周末游客。

——摄影师手记

河北潘家口，2002 年 Panjiakou, Hebei, 2002

From on top of the Wall on one of the islands, I photographed a fisherman sculling over a submerged section of the Wall. Behind him the Wall emerged, climbing the mountainside once again to dominate the landscape before snaking off into the distance.

As I watched him, I wondered how farmers of many generations living in a land-locked province miles from the sea, never having been on a boat and never learning to swim, could suddenly adapt to life on a huge lake. But adapt they did, and fishing seems to have been more desirable, and more profitable, than farming for most. And the lake, the many fish restaurants and the Wall itself are an added boon, drawing weekend tourists from Beijing.

——Photographer's Notes

河北潘家口，2002 年 Panjiakou, Hebei, 2002

北京司马台，2001 年 Simatai, Beijing, 2001

北京，1982 年 Beijing, 1982

北京红螺寺庙会，2002年 Hongluo Temple Fair, Beijing, 2002

北京红螺寺庙会，2002 年 Hongluo Temple Fair, Beijing, 2002

北京明十三陵，2004 年 Ming Tombs, Beijing, 2004

内蒙古元上都遗址，1998 年 Site of Xanadu, Inner Mongolia, 1998

山西偏关老营镇，2002 年 Shanxi Laoying Town, Shanxi, 2002

山西偏关老营镇窑洞，2002 年 Cave House, Shanxi Laoying Town, Shanxi, 2002

山西偏关县寺儿沟长城，2002 年　Siergou Great Wall, Pianguan County, Shanxi, 2002

甘肃山丹峡口，2002 年　Shandan Xiakou, Gansu, 2002

山西大同宁鲁村，2002 年　Ninglu Village, Datong, Shanxi, 2002

山西，2002 年 Shanxi, 2002

山西古村落，2002 年　Ancient Villages, Shanxi, 2002

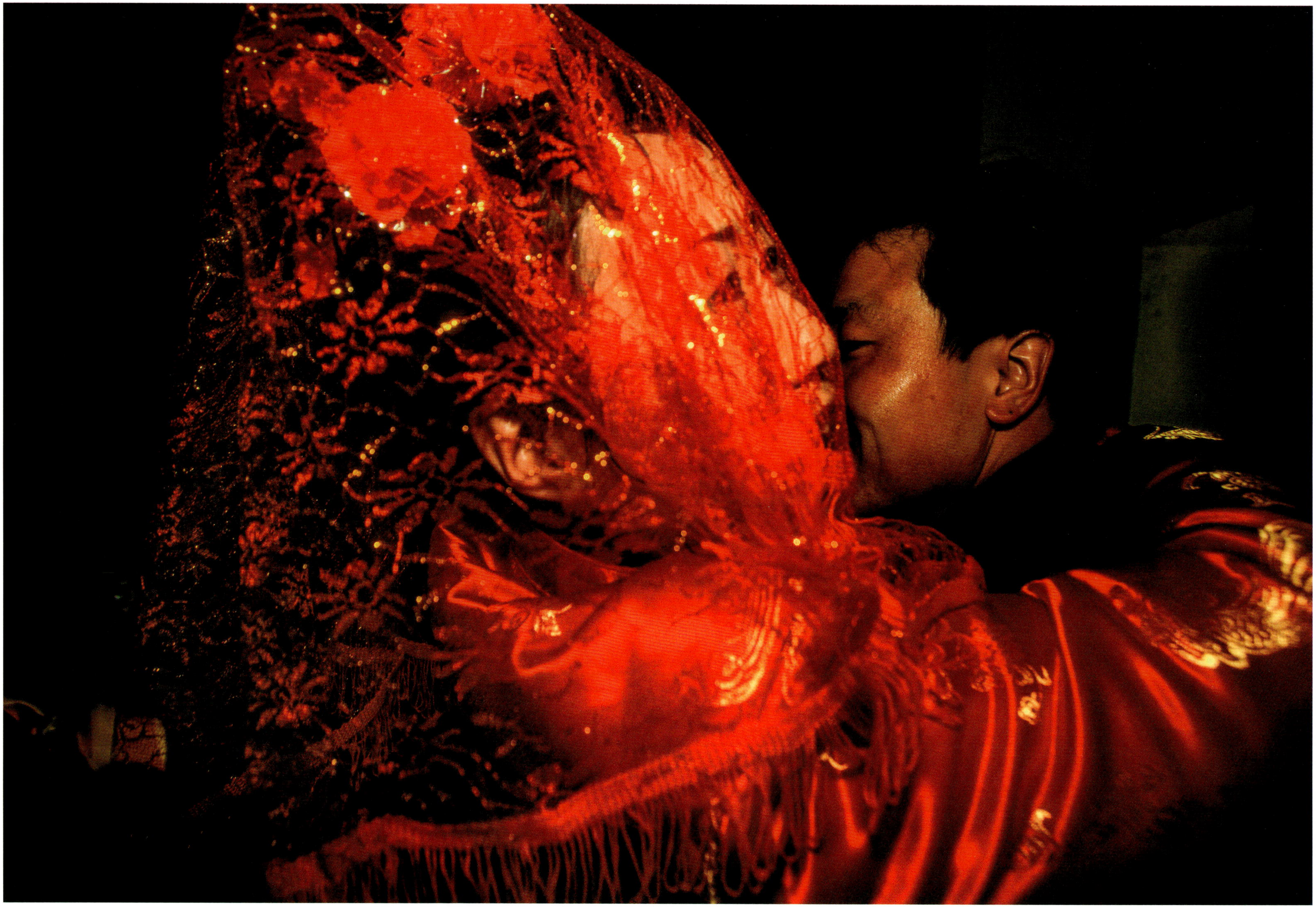

山西大同得胜堡，2004 年　Deshengbao Village, Datong, Shanxi, 2004

山西，2004 年 Shanxi, 2004

陕西佳县黄土高坡，2001 年 Loess Plateau, Jia County, Shaanxi, 2001

宁夏盐池县盐场，2001 年　Salt Factory near Yanchi County, Ningxia, 2001

宁夏 / 内蒙交界处，2001 年　Ningxia / Inner Mongolia Border, 2001

宁夏灵武水洞沟，2001 年 Shuidonggou, Lingwu City, Ningxia, 2001

宁夏，2002 年　Ningxia, 2002

甘肃乌鞘岭—宁夏秦家沟段，2001 年　Enroute from Wushaoling, Gansu to Qinjiagou, Ningxia, 2001

春天来了，是时候去探寻另一段长城了。我选择向北进入内蒙古，去看看更古老的秦代、金代长城还有怎样的遗存。沿途经过的几处长城遗址中，第一处，四子王旗，并没有所谓的『墙』。金长城是一条在地面开挖的堑壕，掘出来的土被用作夯筑一道近两米高的土垒。这种壕沟兼土墙的工事旨在阻止蒙古人骑马冲锋；它是这片平坦草原上最高、最坚硬的地物。经过千年的风雨侵蚀，如今它只剩下不到一尺高的土丘。

——**摄影师手记**

甘肃乌鞘岭，2001 年 Wushaoling, Gansu, 2001

It was now spring – time to check out another section of the Wall. I chose to head north into Inner Mongolia to see what was left of more ancient walls of the Qin and Jin. We were to pass several sites of Qin and Jin Walls, but the first, as Siziwang Qi was not a wall at all. The Jin Wall was a dugout trench, with the displaced soil used to make a six-foot-high compacted earthen barricade. This trench-cum-wall was designed to stop a mounted Mongol's charging horse in his tracks; it was the hardest and highest feature on this flat landscape. Now it has worn to just a hump of no more than a foot high, due to nearly 1,000 years of neglect.

——**Photographer's Notes**

甘肃乌鞘岭，2002 年 Wushaoling, Gansu, 2002

甘肃乌鞘岭，2002 年 Wushaoling, Gansu, 2002

甘肃乌鞘岭，2002 年　Wushaoling, Gansu, 2002

恰逢春季套马，我坐在一辆摩托车的后座上，用我最长焦距的镜头捕捉马儿全速奔跑的画面，它们躲避着牧马人手中挥舞的套马杆。一旦套住马匹，牧马人就会拽住马的尾巴，将其按倒在地。那天早上我目睹的马术表演，足以让我相信中国古代北方游牧民族在战场上的骁勇善战。

——**摄影师手记**

甘肃山丹，2002 年 Shandan, Gansu, 2002

It was time for the spring round-up. From the back of a Chinese motorcycle, I used my longest lenses to capture the horses at full gallop, as they dodged and ran to avoid the looped bamboo poles the tunic-clad herdsmans wielded to lasso them. Once roped and caught, the horses were wrestled to the ground by their tails. The display of horsemanship I witnessed that morning was enough to convince me of the prowess of the nomadic tribes of ancient northern China on the battlefield.

——**Photographer's Notes**

甘肃山丹军马场，2002 年 Shandan' s Army Horse Farm, Gansu , 2002

甘肃嘉峪关，2000 年　Jiayuguan, Gansu, 2000

甘肃金塔县东坝镇，2004 年　Dongba Town, Jinta County, Gansu, 2004

甘肃阳关，2001 年 Yangguan, Gansu, 2001

JOINT EFFORTS
OF GENERATIONS

世代相守

长城是中国古代文明的杰出象征，也是人类历史中的文化遗产。本篇章聚焦长城的建筑与生态保护工作，展示了人们如何代代相传地守护这一世界遗产。得益于政府的保护措施和地方社区的积极参与，长城才能历经岁月洗礼在今天展露新姿。与此同时，沿线的生态保护也同样得到重视，长城两侧的山川河流和生物多样性被悉心保护。本篇章突出了长城在现代化进程中的历史价值与生态价值，强调了文化遗产保护与自然生态保护的紧密联系。

The Great Wall is an icon of ancient Chinese civilization and a cultural heritage of human history. This chapter focuses on the efforts to preserve the Great Wall and the surrounding ecosystem, illustrating how people have protected this world heritage from generation to generation. Thanks to the government's protective measures and the active participation of local communities, the Great Wall has withstood the test of time and now displays a renewed look. Meanwhile, ecological conservation along the Great Wall has also received equal attention, and the mountains, rivers, and biodiversity on both sides of the Wall have been properly safeguarded. This chapter highlights the historical and ecological value of the Great Wall amid modernization and emphasizes the close connection between cultural heritage preservation and nature conservation.

天津长城砖窑厂，2001 年 Great Wall Brick Kilns, Tianjin, 2001

天津长城砖窑厂，2001 年 Great Wall Brick Kilns, Tianjin, 2001

天津长城砖窑厂，2001 年　Great Wall Brick Kilns, Tianjin, 2001

清晨或傍晚的光线，让长城显得格外非凡，砖石在阳光下呈现出温暖的光泽，砖块由灰转成金黄。我在前往那鲜为人知、更加偏远且未经修复的长城段落（所谓的野长城）时，所要寻找的正是这样的光线。

——摄影师手记

北京司马台长城，2003 年 Simatai Great Wall, Beijing, 2003

It is that early morning or late afternoon light that makes the Wall extraordinary as the brick takes on a warm glow, changing the grey brick to golden yellow. This was the light I was looking for as I made my way toward the lesser known, more remote unreconstructed stretch – the so-called Wild Wall.

——Photographer's Notes

北京司马台长城，2003 年 Simatai Great Wall, Beijing, 2003

北京黄花城水长城，2004 年

Huanghuacheng Lakeside Great Wall, Beijing, 2004

山西老牛湾，2002 年　Laoniuwan, Shanxi, 2002

保护母亲

老牛湾位于山西和内蒙古交界处的黄河弯道上，历经数百年狂风侵袭、河水冲刷，这里峭壁陡立，景色壮观。村子三面环水，到河床的垂直落差有七十多米，因此不需要修建围墙来抵御侵犯。一座九米多高的信号塔像哨兵一样挺立，四面八方一览无余。我登上塔顶，此处位置绝佳，视线不再被院墙阻挡，可以俯拍小镇人家。早上7点，几乎看不到人影。我不禁奇怪，如果这是一个人口500的小镇，那么大伙儿都去哪儿了？

——**摄影师手记**

山西老牛湾，2002年 Laoniuwan, Shanxi, 2002

Laoniuwan lies in a spectacular setting above a bend in the Yellow River, on the Shanxi/Inner Mongolia border, atop a vertical walled outcropping chiseled by centuries of rushing wind and water. No walls were needed on three sides of the village, as the 240-foot vertical drop to the riverbed would make it impossible to attack. A 30-foot signal tower stood as tall as a sentry, affording an unobstructed view in every direction. I made for the top of that tower for my first location, picking off pictures of the town, looking over walls that normally block the life within from view. Few were stirring at 7 a.m. I had to wonder, if this was a town of 500, where was everybody?

——**Photographer's Notes**

山西老牛湾，2002 年 Laoniuwan, Shanxi, 2002

甘肃瓜州县，2000 年　Guazhou County, Gansu, 2000

修复甘肃嘉峪关长城，2001 年　Restoration of Jiayuguan Great Wall, Gansu, 2001

驱车前往大同，明朝防御体系中设防最坚固的城镇之一。我的第一站是得胜堡，一个四面有城墙的村庄，附近还有另两个堡垒，彼此近在咫尺。得胜堡外，长城以外是干旱的草原，长城以内则是肥沃却脆弱的黄土高原。这种景观是独一无二的，只属于中国。

——**摄影师手记**

修复甘肃嘉峪关长城，2001 年 Restoration of Jiayuguan Great Wall, Gansu, 2001

I drove in the direction of Datong, one of the most heavily fortified towns of the Ming defense systems. My first stop was the walled village of Deshengbao, one of three forts all within a few feet of each other. Outside the Wall beyond Deshengbao are arid grasslands, and on the inside is the fertile but fragile Loess Plateau. This landscape is uniquely Chinese, found nowhere else in the world.

——**Photographer's Notes**

修复甘肃嘉峪关长城，2001 年 Restoration of Jiayuguan Great Wall, Gansu, 2001

甘肃嘉峪关长城，2001 年　Jiayuguan Great Wall, Gansu, 2001

在宁夏，我的运气和准备得到了回报，这里所享有的沙丘风景美誉当之无愧。我还拍摄了明长城最长的一段，连绵近百公里，是黄河以东宁夏与内蒙古之间的边界。沿着中国最著名的古丝绸之路向西行进，我们在武威城外第一次见到了汉长城，这里曾是丝路上的一个重要防御点。嘉峪关是河西走廊（也可能是整个长城）最重要的关隘，根据行进方向的不同，它可以被视作明长城的起点或终点。嘉峪关号称『天下第一雄关』，它的确令人生畏。对于摄影师而言，这座要塞提供了一个恰到好处的戏剧性的拍摄机会，背景是白雪皑皑的山巅。

——摄影师手记

甘肃嘉峪关，2000 年 Jiayuguan, Gansu, 2000

Luck and preparation paid off in Ningxia, which was justly deserving of its reputation for the best sand dune scenery. I also photographed the longest continuous section of the Ming Wall, a 60-mile stretch which forms the border between Ningxia and Inner Mongolia east of the Yellow River. Farther west along China's most famous road, the ancient Silk Road, our first glimpse of the Han Wall came outside the city of Wuwei, once a major fortified stop on the Silk Road. The most important gate at the Hexi Corridor, perhaps the most important on the entire Great wall, Jiayuguan can be considered either the beginning or the end of the Ming Wall, depending on your direction of travel. Jiayuguan translates as "impregnable fortress under heaven," and it is indeed formidable. For a photographer, the fort provides a fittingly dramatic photo op with its forty-foot walls and sixty-foot towers against a backdrop of snow-capped mountain peaks.

——Photographer's Notes

甘肃嘉峪关，2000 年 Jiayuguan, Gansu, 2000

有人告诉我，镇上的人已出门为种树去了。他们正在建设『绿色长城』，一个由政府主导、世界银行资助的占地360余万公顷的项目。这将是一道由树木组成的屏障，覆盖中国西北部约4500公里的范围。建设『绿色长城』是为了改善生态环境、防治沙漠化。这是典型的中国式工程，也是世界上规模最大的生态工程。

——**摄影师手记**

甘肃玉门关，2001年 Yumenguan, Gansu, 2001

Out planting trees for the World Bank, I was told. They were at work on the Green Great Wall, the name given to a nine-million-acre project sponsored by the government and funded by the World Bank. The Green Great Wall is to be a barrier of trees planted in an area covering 2,800 miles across northwest China, in an attempt to push back the encroaching desert dunes just as the Great Wall was built to stem the advance of the Mongol hordes. It is typically Chinese in scope, the largest ecological project in the history of the world.

——**Photographer's Notes**

甘肃敦煌，2000 年 Dunhuang, Gansu, 2000

TOGETHER FOR A BRILLIANT FUTURE

共襄华彩

长城不仅是中国的历史遗产，也成为世界文化交流的重要平台。本篇章展示了围绕长城开展的各类文化活动与跨文化交流。无论是国际游客的聚集，还是文化项目的举办，长城一直是东西方文化交融的舞台。从传统的节庆活动到现代艺术展览，长城见证了多元文化的互动与碰撞。通过影像，我们可以看到不同文化背景的人们如何在这座古老的墙体前交流思想、分享故事，从而让长城不仅是一道历史遗迹，更成为连接世界的文化纽带。

The Great Wall is not only a cultural heritage site of China; it has also become an important platform for global cultural exchange. This chapter presents the various activities and cross-cultural exchanges carried out around the Great Wall. Whether it is a destination attracting international tourists or a popular spot for hosting cultural projects, the Great Wall has always served as a stage for Eastern and Western cultures to integrate. From traditional festivals to modern art exhibitions, the Great Wall has witnessed the interaction and blending of multiple cultures. Through images, we can see how people from different cultural backgrounds exchange ideas and share stories in front of this ancient wall, making the Great Wall not just a historical relic, but a cultural bond connecting the world.

辽宁丹东虎山长城，2001 年 Hushan Great Wall, Dandong, Liaoning, 2001

人们常常问我，《国家地理》摄影师是如何能屡屡拍出精彩照片，讲述一个又一个故事的。业余爱好者往往误以为我们有无限的时间来完成工作。但即使像长城这样的拍摄项目，一年中分配了相对宽裕的十六周，也没有多少时间可浪费在寻找拍摄对象上。我需要在四个月内，经历多变的气候条件和地形，行进近一万公里，几乎穿越整个中国。于是，做功课就变得极为必要。通过研究，我甚至在看到真实场景之前，就对自己想要拍摄的照片了然于胸。这让拍摄过程变得更像是寻找特定目标，而不是碰运气。我不能什么都拍，所以我选择了长城各段的一些代表性主题，将其列在拍摄清单上。然后我开始寻找，并祈祷能在恰当的光线和情境下找到拍摄对象，拍出精彩之作。再加上一点摄影师的运气，我往往能得偿所愿。

——**摄影师手记**

河北山海关，2008年 Shanhaiguan, Hebei, 2008

天下第一關

I am often asked how *National Geographic* photographers get great pictures, time after time, story after story. Amateurs often mistakenly assume it's because we have unlimited time to complete our assignments. But even with the relatively generous sixteen weeks, spread over a year, allotted for a shoot like the Great Wall, there was little time to waste wandering in search of subjects. I needed to cover 6,000 miles, over almost the entire length of China, through variable climatic conditions and terrain, in four months. That's where doing one's homework pays off. Through research, I knew the pictures I wanted to take even before I saw them. This made the process less a hit-or-miss proposition and more a hunt for specific quarry. I couldn't shoot everything, so I chose a few representative subjects in each section of the Wall, and put them on a shoot list. I then began the search and prayed that I'd find my subjects in the right light and right circumstances to make a great picture. And with a little photographer's luck thrown in, I found those pictures more often than not.

——Photographer's Notes

河北山海关，2001 年 Shanhaiguan, Hebei, 2001

天津黄崖关，2002 年　Huangyaguan, Tianjin, 2002

天津黄崖关，2002 年 Huangyaguan, Tianjin, 2002

天津黄崖关，2002 年　Huangyaguan, Tianjin, 2002

82

FINISH
第四届中国·天津黄崖关长城国际马拉松旅游活动开幕
THE OPENING CEREMONY OF 4TH HUANGYAGUAN INTERNATIONAL GREAT WALL MARATHON·A TOURIST EVENT IN TIANJIN
黄崖正關
Enjoy!
Coca-Cola
50

天津黄崖关，2002 年　Huangyaguan, Tianjin, 2002

河北金山岭长城，2002 年　Jinshanling Great Wall, Hebei, 2002

北京怀北国际滑雪场，2002 年 Huaibei International Ski Resort, Beijing, 2002

北京怀北国际滑雪场，2002 年

Huaibei International Ski Resort, Beijing, 2002

北京怀北国际滑雪场，2002 年 Huaibei International Ski Resort, Beijing, 2002

67

这里，恰好有一段长城正在重建。新的城墙拔地而起，不是为了将谁拒之门外，而是要吸引中外游客前来参观，了解中国的历史。在这里，在长城的尽头，我们满怀希望，迎向新的开始。

——摄影师手记

北京怀北国际滑雪场，2002 年 Huaibei International Ski Resort, Beijing, 2002

Here, a section of the wall was being rebuilt. New Walls were going up, not to exclude but to attract foreigners and locals alike to visit and see the history of China. Here at the end of the Wall, we found the promise of a new beginning.

—Photographer's Notes

北京水关长城，2002 年 Shuiguan Great Wall, Beijing, 2002

北京水关长城，2002 年 Shuiguan Great Wall, Beijing, 2002

北京水关长城，2002 年 Shuiguan Great Wall, Beijing, 2002

北京八达岭长城，2001 年 Badaling Great Wall, Beijing, 2001

北京黄花城长城，2001 年　Huanghuacheng Great Wall, Beijing, 2001

甘肃敦煌鸣沙山，2000 年　Mingsha Mountain, Dunhuang, Gansu, 2000

Postscript: Bricks and Stones as Witnesses, Light and Shadow for Eternal Records

When we first discussed *The Travels of Marco Polo* and the exchange of Eastern and Western cultures with the renowned *National Geographic* photographer Michael Yamashita in 2015, no one could have anticipated that our collaboration would become a cultural journey for a decade.

Forty years of quest, millions of photographs, and a decade of combined efforts have culminated in this book, *Encountering the Great Wall*. Although the roar of bricks and stones fades into silence as one closes the book, the dialogue between civilizations will never stop. While the trembling of the bricks transforms into silent verses, the cultural conversations continue to resonate across the mountains and rivers.

Michael Yamashita has dedicated over forty years to composing a "Song of the Great Wall." This work captures the grandeur of the ten-thousand-mile landscape alongside the warmth of the living world. It is imbued with the vicissitudes of ancient history while pulsating with the rhythm of contemporary China. The Great Wall serves as both the main character of this book and a witness to the dialogue between the East and the West. Once, it transmitted military intelligence through beacon fires; today, it reflects civilization through light and shadow. Yamashita walks on Chinese soil with a dual identity that enjoys both "the outsider's sobriety" and "the insider's affection." We marvel at the "defamiliarized beauty" of the Great Wall as captured by his camera. The aesthetic interpretations shaped by Western compositional rules have transformed the Wall from a mere structure of cold stones into an emotional bond connecting the East and the West. His images shed the detachment of grand narratives, offering a genuine, delicate, and reverent perspective. They vividly portray the joys and sorrows of ordinary people, the breath of the land, and the texture of culture, which collectively embody the ideal of "respecting one's own culture while appreciating the cultures of others for the prosperity of human civilization."

Cultural dissemination is never a one-way exportation; it is a mutual exchange that enriches both sides. The notion of "East Meets West" is never limited to a book or an exhibition; it is a symbol of dialogue that transcends regions, languages, and beliefs. This idea profoundly responds to the coexistence of diverse cultures in the age of globalization and constitutes the spiritual resonance amidst the clash of cultures.

On the occasion of the publication of this book, we would like to pay tribute to all those who have made the light and shadow of the Great Wall eternal. We are grateful to have this opportunity to thank Michael Yamashita for his forty years of continuous exploration. His lens is a "visual Silk Road" that bridges the East and the West. We also thank the ordinary people who have lived beneath the Wall and have safeguarded its bricks and stones for generations. Their stories infuse warmth into history. Our gratitude extends to the Reignwood Culture Foundation for its cultural foresight in preserving the roots of civilization, without which it wouldn't be possible to transform the scattered negatives into a systematic collective memory.

Encountering the Great Wall is not the end. We hope these images will traverse mountains and seas, enabling people of diverse races and beliefs to reflect upon one another through the narratives. We believe that when the poems of bricks and stones are heard by the world, the thoroughfare of culture will no longer have boundaries.

Editor's, March 2025

后记：砖石为证 光影长存

2015 年，当我们第一次与《国家地理》著名摄影师麦克·山下先生讨论《马可·波罗游记》和中西方文化交流的话题时，谁都不曾预料，这场合作将成为跨越十年的文化征程。

四十载步履，百万帧光影，十年携手，终凝为这部《遇见长城》。当最后一页画卷合上，砖石的轰鸣归于寂静，但文明的对话永无止息。当书页轻合，砖石的震颤化作无声的诗行，而文明的对话仍在山河间绵延回响。

麦克·山下用四十余年光阴编织出一部“长城之歌”。它既有壮阔的万里山河，亦有温暖的人间烟火；既镌刻着秦砖汉瓦的沧桑，更跃动着当代中国的脉搏。长城，是这部画册的主角，亦是东西对话的见证者。它曾以烽火传军情，今日却以光影鉴文明。麦克·山下始终以“局外人的清醒”与“局内人的温度”双重身份行走于中国大地。我们惊叹于他镜头中长城的“陌生化美感”——那些被西方构图法则重新诠释的审美意趣，让长城不再是冰冷的石墙，而成为连接东西方情感的纽带。他的影像以真实、细腻且充满敬畏的视角褪去宏大叙事的疏离感，转而浸润于普通人的悲欢、土地的呼吸与文化的肌理之中，真正实现了“各美其美，美美与共”的理想。

真正的文化传播从不是单向输出，而是双向滋养。“当东方遇见西方”从来不止于一本书籍或一场展览，它是跨越地域、语言与信仰的对话符号，是全球化时代对多元文化共生的深刻回应，更是文化在碰撞中孕育出的精神共鸣。

值此画册付梓之际，我们要向所有让长城光影永续的人们致敬：

感谢麦克·山下四十年如一日的行走，他的镜头是跨越东西方的“视觉丝路”。

感谢长城脚下世代守护砖石的平凡人，他们的故事让历史有了温度。

感谢华彬文化基金会以文化远见守护文明根脉，令散落的底片终成体系化的集体记忆。

《遇见长城》不是终点。我们期待，这些影像能跨越山海，让不同肤色、不同信仰的人们在故事中照见彼此；我们相信，当砖石的诗篇被世界聆听，文化的通途便再无疆界。

编者 2025 年 3 月

麦克·山下
Michael Yamashita

Photographer Michael Yamashita has been shooting for the *National Geographic* magazine for over 40 years, combining his dual passions of photography and travel. After graduating from Wesleyan University with a degree in Asian studies, he spent seven years in Asia, which became his photographic area of specialty. Upon returning to the US, Yamashita began shooting for the *National Geographic* as well as other American and international magazines and clients.

In addition to Yamashita's focus on Asia, his work has taken him to six continents. Yamashita's particular specialty is in retracing the paths and historical routes of famous travelers resulting in stories on Marco Polo and the Chinese explorer Zheng He covering the land and sea Silk Road, Chamagudao - the Tea Horse Road, the Great Wall of China, and the Mekong River from source to mouth.

Yamashita has published eleven books (most inspired by his 30 *National Geographic* stories): *88: The China Collection; Shangri-La: Along the Tea Road to Lhasa; The Great Wall: From Beginning to End; New York: Flying High, an aerial portrait of Manhattan; Zheng He: Tracing the Epic Voyages of China's Greatest Explorer; Japan: The Soul of a Nation; Marco Polo: A Photographer's Journey; Mekong: A Journey on the Mother of Waters; In the Japanese Garden; A Pictorial Tribute to the U.S. Merchant Marine Academy;* and *Lakes, Peaks and Prairies: Discovering the U.S. Canadian Border.*

While not traveling, Michael Yamashita lives with his family in rural New Jersey, where he maintains a studio and is an active volunteer fireman.

摄影师麦克·山下先生为《国家地理》杂志拍摄照片已逾40年，这一职业完美结合了他对摄影及旅行两者的热情。从卫斯里大学亚洲研究专业毕业后，他在亚洲生活了7年，亚洲这一题材也成为他日后的摄影专业领域。重返美国后，山下先生开始为《国家地理》及其他美国与国际杂志和客户拍摄照片。

除亚洲之外，山下先生的拍摄足迹遍及六大洲。山下先生尤具特色的创作是重游著名旅行家——譬如马可·波罗和中国明朝探险家郑和——的探险路线，记录沿途自然及人文风光。他由此创作出了涵盖陆上与海上丝绸之路、茶马古道、长城和湄公河全程的摄影作品。

山下先生还出版了11本著作（其中多数受他在《国家地理》杂志上发表的30篇作品启发）：《88：中国作品集》、《寻访香格里拉：探索失落的茶马古道》、《长城》、《纽约》（航拍曼哈顿）、《郑和：追溯中国最伟大探险家的史诗之旅》、《日本：国魂》、《马可·波罗：摄影家之旅》、《湄公河：母亲河之旅》、《在日本园林中》、《影集：向美国商船学校致敬》、《湖泊、山峰与草原：美加边界探索》。

不旅行的时候，麦克·山下先生与家人生活在新泽西乡间，他在那里拥有一间工作室，还是一位积极的消防志愿者。